WAR COMES TO WILLY FREEMAN

by
James Lincoln Collier and Christopher Collier

Teacher Guide

Written by
Jean Jamieson

Note

The Dell Yearling paperback edition of the book was used to prepare this guide. The page references may differ in other editions.

Please note: Please assess the appropriateness of this book for the age level and maturity of your students prior to reading and discussing it with your class.

ISBN 1-56137-594-2

To order, contact your local school supply store, or—

Novel Units, Inc.
P.O. Box 433
Bulverde, TX 78163-0433

Web site: www.educyberstor.com

Table of Contents

Skills and Strategies

Thinking
Brainstorming, visualization, research questions, problem-solving

Comprehension
Predicting, comparison/contrast

Listening/Speaking
Discussion, role play, drama, interviewing

Vocabulary
Context clues, synonyms, antonyms

Writing
Poetry, persuasion, narrative, description

Literary Elements
Characterization, story elements, alliteration

Summary

Willy, disguised as a boy, is trapped at Fort Griswold as the British advance. Allowed to escape after the Americans are massacred, her father being among the dead, Willy returns home to find that her mother has been taken to New York City as a British prisoner. Willy starts on a long search for her mother. Finding refuge at the famous Fraunces Tavern, she is continually reminded that being black, female, and free leave her vulnerable and open to constant danger. Although she eventually finds her mother, Willy's troubles and adventures do not end.

(Authors' comments taken from "How Much of This Book Is True?" pages 175-178. "The language used in this book...is almost certainly not how people spoke at the time...We have therefore tried to give something of the flavor of how an uneducated black person might have spoken then...we had to consider very carefully our use of the word *nigger*. This term is offensive to modern readers, and we certainly do not intend to be insulting. But it was commonly used in America right into the twentieth century, and it would have been a distortion of history to avoid its use entirely.")

About the Authors

Christopher Collier was born January 29, 1930 in New York, New York. He married Virginia Wright August 21, 1954. After the marriage ended, he married Binnie Bromberger on December 6, 1969. He attended Clark University, B.A., 1951; Columbia University, M.A., 1955, Ph.D., 1964. His hobbies and other interests include trumpet playing, figure skating, ice hockey, water skiing, and reading.

Mr. Collier has been a high school teacher and a college professor of history. He is a consultant to numerous public and private organizations including museums, historical societies, law firms, public utilities, and text, trade, and scholarly publishers.

James Lincoln Collier was born June 27, 1928, in New York, New York. He was educated at Hamilton College, A.B., 1950. "I have been deeply involved in jazz from youth, and continue to work as a jazz musician regularly."

James and Christopher Collier come from a family of writers. "We all do it because we like to, but we write also as a way of earning a living that makes it possible for us to set our own schedules, take our vacations when we please, and not have to take orders from anyone."

The Colliers fashioned a system of producing books wherein Christopher conceptualizes and provides historical details to the work while James creates the characters and story lines. Christopher chooses something that he wants to teach about, and James makes the stories interesting, exciting, and fun to read. He gives the individuals in the books character and personality. "Collaboration between historians and writers is necessary so that historical fiction can be read with enjoyment and so that history can be learned without young readers thinking that they're being taught history. The author of children's books can deliver more than just a good read, but also a view of the world."

Introductory Information and Activities

Note: Please be selective, and use discretion when choosing the activities that you will do with the unit. Is is not intended that everything be done but that discretionary choices made are most appropriate for your use and group of students. A wide range has been provided, so that individuals as well as groups may benefit from these selections.

Initiating Activity

Make a large banner to hang in the room that has these words on it:

"We hold these Truths to be self-evident, that all Men are created equal."

Have a record or a tape of the song "Yankee Doodle" playing in the background as the students arrive. (See Teacher Information.)

Read aloud to the group "The War Inevitable," March, 1775 by Patrick Henry, which ends with his famous quote, "I know not what course others may take; but as for me, give me liberty or give me death!" (You may want to consider using *I Am What You Make Me [The Flag Speaks]* at the close of this unit, or your present study of the Revolutionary War, if that is the purpose of this selection. The conclusion of the speech, also known as "The War Inevitable," may be found in the encyclopedia. Look up *Patrick Henry*.) Discuss this speech, and the possible reaction(s) to it. How do you think you would have responded to these words?

Bulletin Board Idea

Cover the bulletin board with plain background paper. On it place a banner with these words from Patrick Henry: "Give me liberty or give me death!"

Recommended Procedure

This book may be used in several ways: a) read to the entire class; b) read with the class; c) read in reading groups; d) read individually. The questions and activities at the end of each chapter, as well as any supplementary activities, are provided so that you may, using discretion, make selections from them that will be suitable for use by the students in your group.

Previewing the Book

Have students examine the cover of the book. How would you describe the expression on the face of the girl pictured? (pensive? thoughtful? afraid? apprehensive? calculating? serene?) Why do you think that she looks as she does? What else pictured on the cover would give an indication as to the setting and time in history that the story takes place?

Prereading Activity

Place a large cluster circle on the chalkboard or a large sheet of paper. Brainstorm the word WOMEN. Ask the students to think of words that describe the roles, rights, opportunities, etc., that women had at this time in history. Record the replies. Keep on display, and place additional information on it as more is learned during the reading of the novel.

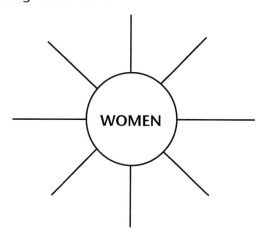

Prereading Discussion

Read the paragraph from the book that starts on page 177 with "The language used in this book is a case in point," and ends on page 178 with, "...the Revolutionary era." Also refer to these quotes from the book:

- Page 109, "That was the way Pa treated my Ma. It was his right. He loved her, but he had a duty to command her, too, and she had a duty to obey."

- Pages 63-64, "Although when I came to think about it, when you was a woman you was half a slave, anyway. You had to get married, otherwise you couldn't hardly support yourself, and after that your husband, he was the boss and you had to do what he said. That was so even for white women: Mrs. Ivers couldn't go against Captain Ivers no more than Ma could go against Pa. And of course, if you was black, you was down at the bottom anyway."

- Page 26, "...but then suddenly it came to me that if I told him I was a girl he'd start giving me orders and maybe wouldn't let me help with the cartridges."

- Page 15, "She wanted to argue with him, but she didn't dare. He was the man, and she had to do what he told her to do."

From these quotes, what do you imagine it was like to be a woman during the time of the Revolutionary War? What is your opinion of the treatment of women during this time in history? Discuss. (Refer also to page 64. Willy is thinking about the reason for the fighting, and thinks that women will be no better off after the war, even if the Americans win.)

Why do you think that Willy Freeman is pictured dressed as a boy on the book's cover?

Using Predictions

We all make predictions as we read—little guesses about what will happen next, how a conflict will be resolved, which details will be important to the plot, which details will help fill in our sense of a character. Students should be encouraged to predict, to make sensible guesses as they read the novel.

As students work on their predictions, these discussion questions can be used to guide them: What are some of the ways to predict? What is the process of a sophisticated reader's thinking and predicting? What clues does an author give to help us make predictions? Why are some predictions more likely to be accurate than others?

Create a chart for recording predictions. This could be either an individual or class activity. As each subsequent chapter is discussed, students can review and correct their previous predictions about plot and characters as necessary.

Use the facts and ideas the author gives.

Use your own prior knowledge.

Apply any new information (i.e., from class discussion) that may cause you to change your mind.

Predictions

_____

_____

_____

_____

Prediction Chart

What characters have we met so far?	What is the conflict in the story?	What are your predictions?	Why did you make those predictions?

Using Character Webs

Attribute webs are simply a visual representation of a character from the novel. They provide a systematic way for students to organize and recap the information they have about a particular character. Attribute webs may be used after reading the novel to recapitulate information about a particular character, or completed gradually as information unfolds. They may be completed individually or as a group project.

One type of character attribute web uses these divisions:

- How a character acts and feels. (How does the character act? How do you think the character feels? How would you feel if this happened to you?)

- How a character looks. (Close your eyes and picture the character. Describe him/her to me.)

- Where a character lives. (Where and when does the character live?)

- How others feel about the character. (How does another specific character feel about our character?)

In group discussion about the characters described in student attribute webs, the teacher can ask for backup proof from the novel. Inferential thinking can be included in the discussion.

Attribute webs need not be confined to characters. They may also be used to organize information about a concept, object, or place.

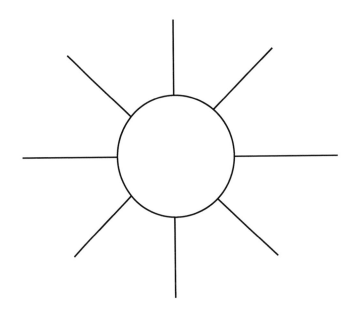

Attribute Web

The attribute web below will help you gather clues the author provides about a character in the novel. Fill in the blanks with words and phrases which tell how the character acts and looks, as well as what the character says and what others say about him or her.

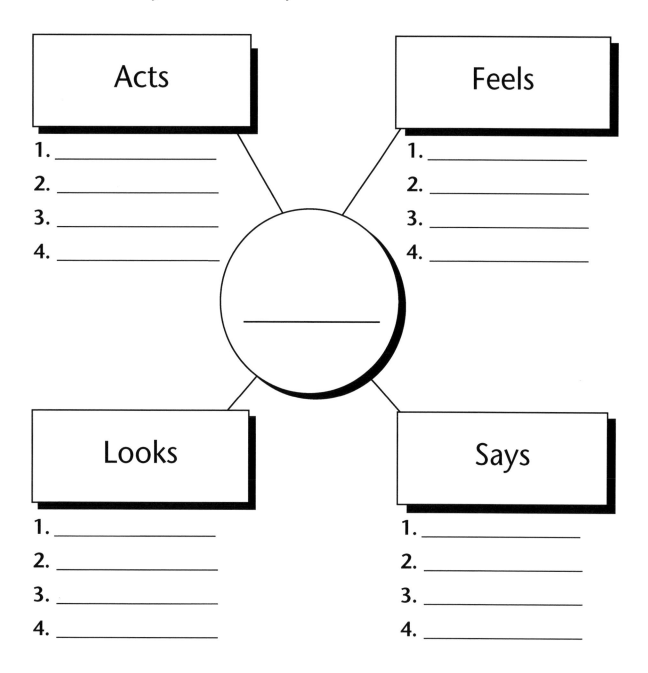

Story Map

Characters_____

_____

```
┌─────────────┐
│   Setting   │
└─────────────┘
       │
       ▼
┌─────────────┐
│   Problem   │
└─────────────┘
       │
       ▼
┌─────────────┐
│    Goal     │
└─────────────┘
       │
       ▼
┌─────────────┐
│  Episodes   │
└─────────────┘
       │
       ▼
┌─────────────┐
│ Resolution  │
└─────────────┘
```

Time and Place_____

_____

Problem_____

_____

_____

Goal_____

_____

_____

Beginning ⟶ Development ⟶ Outcome

_____

_____

_____

_____

Resolution_____

_____

_____

_____

Chapter 1—Pages 1-11

To the Teacher: Please read the section "How Much of This Book Is True?" (Pages 175-178) before starting the unit.

Vocabulary

bayonets 1	determined 2	jolly boat 2	militia 2
britches 3	smithereens 4	amongst 5	squinch 5
tether 5	straggling 6	rebels 10	

Vocabulary Activity

Use a vocabulary word to complete each sentence.

1. Willy wears special _____ when she milks the cow. *(britches)*

2. Willy's father has a _____ for fishing. *(jolly boat)*

3. The cannon ball could smash the boat to _____ . *(smithereens)*

4. _____ fit on the ends of guns. *(Bayonets)*

5. Willy left the cow on her _____ after milking. *(tether)*

6. Willy was _____ to help her parents. *(determined)*

7. The jolly boat was on the water _____ the British fleet. *(amongst)*

8. Willy's father joined the _____ . *(militia)*

Discussion Questions and Activities

1. Who is telling the story? *(Page 3, Wilhelmina Freeman, called Willy, is telling the story.)* How old is Willy? *(Page 3, Willy is 13 years old.)* (See Supplementary Activity #1.)

2. How does Willy's father get his freedom? *(Page 2, Jordan Freeman gets his freedom by joining the militia. By law, if a black slave was going to join up to fight the British, he had to be set free first.)* How do Willy and her mother get their freedom? *(Page 2, Colonel Ledyard gives Willy and her mother their freedom, too.)* What is your opinion of Colonel Ledyard because of this act?

3. Why is Willy scared on the day that the story starts? *(Page 1, British soldiers are marching past their cabin, with bayonets fixed to their guns.)* Willy and Ma stand in front of their cabin and watch the soldiers go past. What do you think that you would do in that situation? How do you think that you would feel?

4. What chore does Willy have to do? What does she have to wear? Why? *(Pages 3-4, Willy has to milk the cow. Since her mother does not want anyone seeing her legs, Willy has to put on milking breeches in order to sit on the milking stool to milk the cow.)* (See Supplementary Activity #2.)

5. What happens to the cow? *(Page 7, Two black soldiers kill the cow.)* What do the soldiers tell

Mrs. Freeman after they see that she is black? *(Page 7, They tell Mrs. Freeman that they would have left the cow alone. "We ain't supposed to bother the black folk.")* Why are the soldiers ordered not to bother black folks? *(Page 9, The British generals think that the black people will fight on their side if they are treated nicely. Some black people, such as the soldiers who killed the cow, already feel that they will continue to be slaves if the Americans win.)* How do you think that the black people in the Colonies must be feeling about themselves and their futures at this time in history?

Supplementary Activities

1. Start a character attribute web for Willy. Add to it as the story continues. (See pages 8-9 of this guide.)

2. You are a reporter for the local newspaper. Your editor has furnished you with a newly developed laser screen that is able to bring to the current times people of the past to interview. Mrs. Freeman, Willy's mother, is the person that you are assigned to interview. Your editor wants the readers of the newspaper to have Mrs. Freeman's opinion of the current fashions. Write out the questions that you will ask her, and then record her answers. Since the photographer is on assignment elsewhere, it is also up to you to furnish the illustrations for your interview.

3. On page 6 the author describes some of the "awful noise" that the British troops are making. "The cannon wheels was rumbling, the axles squeaking, and the drums rat-tat-tatting..." What else might be making a noise? What sound would it be making? Think of additional things and sounds. Make a list, and then compile the information. How many different kinds of noises are listed?

4. The chapter ends on page 11. Reread the last short paragraph on that page. What do you predict will happen next? Record the prediction, and verify it as the next chapter is read.

Chapter 2—Pages 13-21

Vocabulary

swiveled 13	sockets 14	argumentative 14	hoisted 15
tacking 16	cockade 17	calculating 20	musket ball 21

Vocabulary Activity

How many words can you make from the letters in the word argumentative in three minutes? *(For example: men, ten, man, tan, ran, time, grime, mine, gave, rave, gum, tag, rag, nag, vine, give, rat, mat, mate, rate, gate, tame, name, game, mug, rug, tug, mean, teen, ream...)*

Discussion Questions and Activities

1. Why is Willy to go to the fort with Pa? *(Page 17, Willy is to go so that she can bring the horse back home.)* Do you think that it is important that the horse get back home? Why do you think about it as you do?

2. How is Willy dressed? *(Page 17, Willy still has on the milking breeches and a shirt. Her father has given her one of his hats to wear, and he tells Willy, "With them britches on, you look like a boy, anyway.")* Do you think that it is best for Willy that she looks like a boy? Why? Why not?

3. How does Pa get into the fort? *(Pages 20-21, Someone inside the fort lets down a rope, and Pa is pulled up headfirst over the wall.)* What words would you use to describe Willy's father?

Supplementary Activities

1. Role play the scene in which Mrs. Freeman begs Mr. Freeman not to go to Fort Griswold. It starts at the top of page 17 with, "Pa jumped up," and ends at the top of page 18 with, "I didn't dare go against him."

2. After Willy sees that Pa is in the fort, she goes to take the horse home. As she rides off, some British soldiers come through the woods, directly toward her (page 21). The chapter ends with, "My eyes was closed and all I could think was that any second a musket ball could catch me in the back." Make some predictions. What will happen to Willy? What will happen to Pa? What is going on at home with Ma?

Chapter 3—Pages 23-31

Vocabulary

palisades 24	barracks 24	massacre 25	magazine 25
cartridges 26	pikes 29		

Vocabulary Activity

Make up a tongue twister using the vocabulary words *magazine, massacre,* and other words that begin with the letter **M**. Begin by adding a third word to the vocabulary words, to make the first tongue twister three words long. When able to say that fast three times, add another word to the twister. Continue adding on until the tongue twister is five or six words long. For example:

Moronic Magazine Massacre

Mean Moronic Magazine Massacre

Malicious Mean Moronic Magazine Massacre

Misguided Malicious Mean Moronic Magazine Massacre

Discussion Questions and Activities

1. What happens to Willy? *(Page 24, Willy heads back to the fort, is given the rope, and is pulled to safety by Pa.)* Willy thinks that she is now safe. Do you agree with her? Why or why not?

2. What is the significance of the white flag being held by the British officers? *(Pages 24-25, The white flag is used to signal a request for a cease fire. The British want to tell the men in the fort that if they do not surrender, there will be a massacre.)* What is the reply from the fort? *(Page 25, They are going to fight.)* Do you think that this is a wise decision? (See Supplementary Activity #1.)

3. Where in the fort is Willy sent by Pa? What is she to do? *(Page 26, Willy is sent to the powder magazine, a small room, to help to make cartridges, ammunition.)* Why can't there be any lanterns in the magazine? *(Page 26, There are no lanterns because of the barrels of gunpowder in the magazine. The lanterns burn kerosene as a fuel. The heat and flame could be dangerous near gunpowder.)* Do you think that Willy is safe working in the magazine? Where in the fort would you choose to be? Why?

4. Why does Willy leave the magazine? *(Page 29, Willy goes to deliver cartridges to the men.)* Does Willy get the cartridges delivered? Why? *(Page 29, No. She drops the basket holding the cartridges. The British have gotten into the fort, and are killing all of the Americans.)* What does Willy do? *(Page 30, Willy crouches down into a corner of the palisades.)* What do you imagine that Willy is thinking as she hides?

5. Willy looks for Pa (page 30). Refer back to the top of page 5. Earlier in the day Willy was also thinking about her father. "I began to think about if he would really fight, the way Ma said, and what that would be like. What would it be like to get stabbed by a bayonet?" What happens to Pa? *(Page 30, Pa is killed. Willy sees a bayonet go through her father's back.)* Do you imagine that thinking about this happening earlier has helped Willy face the reality of it actually happening? Discuss. (See Supplementary Activity #2, and Post-reading Activity, Fort Griswold.)

Supplementary Activities

1. What if the men in Fort Griswold did decide to surrender? What do you think would happen to them? A change in circumstance changes the story. Write a group story about the surrender of Fort Griswold. Dramatize the story.

2. The chapter ends on page 31 with this sentence: "The shouting and the killing went on and on, and I crouched there on the platform with my eyes closed, crying and moaning and waiting to be killed." Do you know a folk song, or a poem that might help Willy express her feelings, or in which she might find some comfort? Do you want to create some music or poetry to help her? Use music and/or poetry to help Willy in some way. For example:

Grief
by Jean Jamieson

The gigantic hands of grief shake me and batter me about.

They toss me against the wall, turning me inside out.

They lift me up and again get ready for another toss.

How can they do this to me? How can I face this loss?

But the hands, they are unrelenting, grasping tighter yet,

They let fly, and I travel in dark despair swiftly, like a jet

Soaring first, then plummeting to the ground with a fiery crash.

The hands gather up my bones and bury them with my ash.

Chapter 4—Pages 33-46

Vocabulary

hither and yon 35   frigates 39   gunnel 42   dwindled 43

Vocabulary Activity

Define the vocabulary words/phrase. Use each word/phrase in a sentence. Illustrate one of the sentences. *(For Your Information: Gunnel—a piece of timber around the top side of a boat and having oarlocks for the oars; hither and yon—near and far/here and there)*

Discussion Questions and Activities

1. Why do you think that the British soldier allows Willy to leave the fort? *(Page 33, Answers will vary.)*

2. As Willy approaches the family cabin she thinks, "It (the cabin) was just the same, but everything else was changed, and nothing would ever be the same again" (page 36). What do you think that Willy means by that?

3. Where is Ma? *(Page 38, Granny Hyde tells Willy that her mother has been taken to New York by the British.)* What does Willy decide to do? *(Page 41, Willy decides to walk to Stratford to her Aunt Betsy.)* Do you think that Willy makes a wise decision? Why or why not? (See Supplementary Activity #1.)

4. Does Willy have to walk to Stratford? *(Page 41, No. Pa's jolly boat is still where he left it, so Willy decides to sail to Stratford.)* How long does it take her to get there? *(Page 43, She sails all day.)* What words can you add to Willy's attribute web? (See Supplementary Activities #2 and #3.)

5. What kind of a welcome does Willy get from Aunt Betsy and her family? *(Pages 45-46, Willy is received warmly. She thinks, "I was mighty glad that I'd come there.")* How do you think that Willy feels at the end of that day?

Supplementary Activities

1. When making her plans to go to Stratford, Willy thinks that she could probably walk the 50 miles in three days. How many miles per day would she have to walk to do this? *(Willy would have to walk approximately 17 miles per day, [16.67], to get to Stratford in three days.)* Approximately how many hours would it take her to walk the 17 miles at a rate of 2 miles per hour? *(8.5 hours; distance = rate x time)*

Fill in the following table:

Distance to Travel	Rate (mph)	Time (approx.)
17 miles	3 miles per hour	*(6 hours [5.67]) ans.*
17 miles	3.5 miles per hour	*(5 hours [4.86]) ans.*
20 miles	*(2 miles per hour) ans.*	10 hours
24 miles	*(4 miles per hour) ans.*	6 hours
(28 miles) ans.	4 miles per hour	7 hours

Fill in at least three additional spaces, giving the distance, rate, and time.

2. Get a map of Connecticut. Using the scale given on your map, figure the approximate distance that Willy sails in the jolly boat from her home to Stratford. *(Page 3, "We lived out on a little spit of land that bordered on the Thames River, where it ran into Long Island Sound.")* After you have obtained the information, convert the statute miles to nautical miles. You will need the following information: There are 5,280 feet in a statute mile; there are 6,080 feet in a nautical mile. For example: If the information obtained from the map is 50 (statute) miles, multiply that by 5,280 to get the total number of feet, 264,000. To find out how many nautical miles that would be, divide 264,000 by 6,080, 43.42. Therefore, if Willy walks she would travel 50 statute miles; if she sails on the water, she would travel 43.42 nautical miles.

Keep that map, and one of New York handy so that Willy's travels may be plotted. (The maps pictured in the encyclopedia, Connecticut and New York, will be sufficient for this purpose.)

3. Start a story map about Willy's search for her mother. (See page 10 of this guide.)

Chapter 5—Pages 47-58

Vocabulary

furloughed 47   curtsy 48   skirmishing 52   suspicious 56

Vocabulary Activity

(Furlough: Leave of absence; vacation) Write a persuasive paragraph in which you explain why you should be granted a "furlough" (i.e., be furloughed) from doing something for a week, such as taking out the garbage, cleaning your room, etc. How persuasive can you be? Share with the group. (Perhaps the group, or a "panel of experts" would decide whether or not they would grant you the "furlough," if it was in their power to do so.)

Discussion Questions and Activities

1. How is Willy treated by Captain and Mrs. Ivers? *(Page 53, Willy is treated like a slave. However, Willy knows that she will have to do as she is told in order to stay with Aunt Betsy, and to avoid punishment.)* What advice would you give Willy for getting along with people like Captain and Mrs. Ivers?

2. Mrs. Ivers tells Aunt Betsy on page 51, "This is a God-fearing home..." *(God-fearing: religious)* In your opinion, do Captain and Mrs. Ivers' actions and treatment of others seem to be the kind that one would expect in a "God-fearing home"? (Are they considerate of others? Are they helpful? Are they kind?)

3. Why does Willy feel that she cannot stay with Aunt Betsy for too long? *(Page 51, Willy thinks that Captain Ivers is going to figure out a way to put her back into slavery.)* What are Willy's plans? *(Page 52, Willy wants to take the jolly boat and go to New York to look for her mother.)* Do Aunt Betsy and Uncle Jack agree to these plans? *(Page 54, No. Uncle Jack tells Willy that it is too risky for her to go to New York.)* What do you think? Should Willy go to New York or stay in Stratford? Why? Record the opinions. See the following page for an example:

STRATFORD		NEW YORK
Reasons for Staying	**Reason for Leaving**	**Reasons for Going to New York**
Family	Captain & Mrs. Ivers	Look for Ma
Food shortage in New York	Possible slavery	Get away from the Ivers
Place to stay	Ill treatment	More freedom

4. What does Willy decide to do? *(Page 55, Willy decides to go to New York in the jolly boat.)* Think of one thing that you think that Willy should take along with her to New York. Compile a list. Review the things listed. Remember that Willy is going in the jolly boat, which is not very large. Also, she has no place to stay when she gets to New York. What things from the list do you think are absolutely necessary for Willy to take? What should she leave behind? Discuss. Make a group decision.

Supplementary Activities

1. Compare Aunt Betsy and Mrs. Ivers. Use a T-chart for ease of comparison. For example:

Aunt Betsy	**Mrs. Ivers**
Kind	Thin
Welcoming	Pointed nose
Gentle	Stares
Gives hugs	Unkind
Does not trust Captain Ivers	Demanding

Add to the comparison as more is learned about the characters. What conclusions may be made with regard to these two women to date?

2. Brainstorm the word SLAVE. (See Teacher Information section, Slaves for America.)

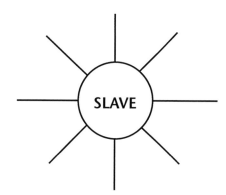

3. Before Willy leaves for New York, she takes a good look at Aunt Betsy's face so that she will be able to remember what her aunt looks like. Think of the face of someone that you care about. Paint a picture of that face with words. You may use prose or poetry. For example:

Smooth. White, with freckles placed here and there.
A few wrinkles etched by time, but oh so truly fair.
Smiles freely given from a mouth with words so kind.
A gentle, caring face. The best friend one could find.

4. As Willy is sailing in the jolly boat to New York, she sees five or six whaleboats that turn and head toward her (page 58). What do you think will happen next? Make a prediction.

Chapter 6—Pages 59-69

Vocabulary
hunkered 59   keel 62   clapboard 67

Vocabulary Activity
The word *hunkered* is used in the following sentence in the book. "Just then one of the men hunkered down beside me, his face so close to mine I could hear him breathe and see the whites of his eyes shine in the starlight." What are some different words that could be substituted in the sentence and still retain the meaning of it? *(crouched, knelt, sat...)*

Discussion Questions and Activities
1. Willy is captured. Why isn't she thrown overboard? *(Pages 60-61, Willy tells the men about the battle at Fort Griswold, the attempt of Colonel Ledyard to surrender, and of her father's death. This coincides with what is known by the men.)* What kinds of feelings do you think that Willy has inside as all of this is happening?

2. As Willy is thinking about why the fighting is going on, she likens it to children growing up (page 64). What does she think? *("The way it looked to me, the Americans—least-wise the white men—figured they was grown up and shouldn't have to do what the British told them; and the British figured the Americans wasn't grown up and ought to obey. That was what the war was about. But no matter who won, it wouldn't leave the slaves no better off, nor the women, neither.")* What changes do you think that the slaves and women would like to have made? Use a Venn diagram to record your suggestions. The overlap is for recording changes that both the slaves and women would like to have made.

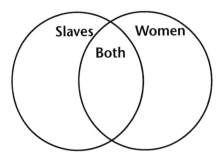

Supplementary Activities

1. Willy stands on a low bluff and looks across the river at New York (page 68). Using the art media of your choice, make an illustration of the scene that Willy experiences as she stands on that bluff. You may decide to include only the view of the land itself, or only the prison ships anchored in the bay rather than the entire scene.

2. Willy sees buildings in New York that are five stories high. Locate some things in your environment that are approximately five stories high. (Allow approximately 10 feet per story when locating things of similar height.) Visually compare something that is approximately five stories high to other things in your environment. Are they as tall as, shorter than, or about the same height? Some suggestions: water tower, flag pole, oak tree, telephone pole, high tension wire tower, etc. If possible, measure the shadow that is cast by at least one of the objects at different times of the day. What conclusions may be made when the results are compared? Would comparing the size of shadows of different objects help you in knowing more about the size comparisons of the objects themselves?

Chapter 7—Pages 71-76; Chapter 8—Pages 77-90

Vocabulary

ferry 77	cordwood 78	tuppence 78	refugees 81
loyalists 81	populace 86		

Vocabulary Activity

Use the word *ferry* in a limerick. A limerick is a light humorous or nonsensical verse of five lines, usually with the rhyme scheme of aabba. For example:

> *There once was a ferry of sorts*
> *That traveled between two far-off ports.*
> *Passengers, though few at the dock*
> *Were always in for quite a shock*
> *For the ferryman wore only his shorts.*

Discussion Questions and Activities

1. Why does Willy go to the dock? *(Page 73, Willy wants to ask the British soldiers if there are any black women on board the prison ships. She is looking for her mother.)* Do you think that Willy is brave or foolish to do this? Why?

2. How does Willy get from Long Island to New York City? *(Pages 82-83, Willy gets a ride with Horace, who is carrying cordwood in a wagon for Sam Fraunces. When they get close to the ferry, Willy hides among the wood in the wagon. When they get ashore, Willy rides up front with Horace to the Fraunces' tavern.)* What do you think of Willy's good fortune on that day? Does it continue? *(Pages 88-90, Yes. Willy is given food at the tavern, and then tells her story to Sam Fraunces. She is allowed to stay, as a boy, and to work at the tavern.)* Why do you think that Willy hesitates to tell Mr. Fraunces that she is an American? Do you think that she knows if he sides with the British or the Americans at the close of this chapter? What do you think about Sam Fraunces?

Supplementary Activities

1. Do some research. Find out more about the prison ships used by the British during the war. *(Prison Ships: The British used large old ships called hulks and converted them to prisons. The ships were stripped of sails and fittings and the portholes were boarded up. There were small slits cut in the sides of the ships for air, but otherwise the prisoners were completely sealed in. The hulks were ghastly, filthy places, and hundreds of men were crowded into rooms that would be cramped quarters for 20. When they received any food at all, it was rotten and crawling with insects. The water was greenish-yellow in color, and had a foul, sour smell. Rats were everywhere, and with the rats came disease. Smallpox, yellow fever, and severe diarrhea were common. Because of the crowding, disease spread quickly. Each morning the prisoners were told to "turn out the dead," and the Americans hoisted up the bodies of the men who had died during the night. Prisoners were allowed to ascend to the deck in the morning, and viewed a boat loaded with dead bodies being taken ashore for burial. The prison ships killed more than 13,000 Americans during the war. The Old Jersey was known as the worst. Eleven thousand men, more than the total killed in George Washington's army, died aboard that ship.)*

2. Read about James Forten, who survived a stay on the Jersey and went on to become one of the wealthiest men in Philadelphia.

Chapter 9—Pages 91-105

Vocabulary

cipher 92   sawyers 93   apothecary 95

Vocabulary Activity

(Cipher: [as used in the context of the story] to solve problems in arithmetic; calculate) Have each student make up 10 problems to solve. Make a composite of these, for example by taking the first of each, and give the composite to the group to solve. (See Post-reading Activities, Cipher Continued.)

Discussion Questions and Activities

1. Willy and Horace get some time off from work. Where do they go? Why? *(Pages 96-99, They go to Canvas Town to look for Willy's mother.)* What do they see in Canvas Town? Would you like to be there with them? (See Supplementary Activity #1.)

2. On page 100, Horace has some advice for her when Willy asks his opinion about the truthfulness of what they were told by the woman in Canvas Town. What does Horace tell Willy? *(Horace tells Willy that she should think for herself; make her own decisions after thinking things through very carefully.)* What is your opinion of the advice that Horace gives to Willy?

3. Do Willy and Horace return to Canvas Town that night? What do they find? *(Pages 103-104, Yes. The woman who told them about Willy's mother is dead.)* How do you think they are feeling as they run off? Do you think that they used good judgment in returning to Canvas Town that night? Why or why not?

Supplementary Activities

1. The streets in Canvas Town are described as being a field of mud, deep and thick (page 95). When people die, their bodies are just pushed down into the mud. "You could walk on dead bodies from one side of Canvas Town to the other" (page 96). Use mud as the theme for something that you create. You may wish to use art media, music, poetry, or prose to describe the mud in some way, and what happens to it in a specific situation.

2. Towns often have special signs that welcome people, and tell something about the town, such as: Welcome To Our Town; The Home of Good Neighbors; We Have What You Want.

   Make a sign for Canvas Town.

Chapter 10—Pages 107-119

Vocabulary

bargaining 108   scoundrels 108   instructive 109

Vocabulary Activity

Develop word maps for the vocabulary words. Follow the form given.

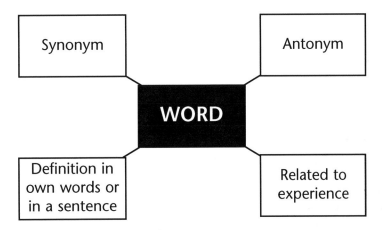

Discussion Questions and Activities

1. Why do you think that Willy finds masquerading as a boy very "instructive"? *(Page 109, Willy mentions some things that she notices that she does not have to do, such as having Horace boss her around so that she has to fetch his meals, check the water of the chickens, and do other lowly tasks which they now share.)*

2. Do you think that the relationship between Horace and Willy will change, now that Horace knows that Willy is a girl (page 118)? If so, what changes might occur? List possible changes. Check them out as the story continues.

Supplementary Activities

1. Horace, if he does say so himself, seems to be able to do many things very well. In this chapter, page 115, he says that he is a wonderful swimmer. Think of something different for Horace to excel in, and write about a situation in which he will be able to brag about it.

2. Make a prediction. If Horace tries to boss her around, will Willy do as she is told? On what do you base your prediction?

Chapter 11—Pages 121-132

Vocabulary

leastwise 121	negotiations 123	sauntering 124	fritter 124
jollity 127			

Vocabulary Activity

Complete each of the following comparisons using a vocabulary word. (*Example*: GOOD is to BAD as HOT is to COLD.)

1. GLAD is to HAPPY as _____ is to ANYWAY.   *(LEASTWISE)*

2. MORE is to LESS as _____ is to SAVE.   *(FRITTER)*

3. UNHAPPY is to SAD as _____ is to MERRIMENT.   *(JOLLITY)*

4. GOOD is to KIND as _____ is to STROLLING.   *(SAUNTERING)*

5. NIGHT is to DARK as _____ is to DISCUSSIONS.   *(NEGOTIATIONS)*

Discussion Questions and Activities

1. Check your prediction with the information given on page 124. How did you do?

2. Willy and Horace get paid for working at the tavern. What do they do with the money that they earn? *(Pages 125-126, Horace saves his money. Willy has a sweet tooth, and spends most of her money on goodies at the shop of Mr. Joseph Corre.)* Do you think that you would be like Horace or Willy with your earnings? If you spent your money, what would you purchase? If you saved your money, what would be your goal?

3. What decision does Willy make regarding Ma? *(Page 130, Willy decides that the best thing is to forget about trying to find Ma, and to look out for herself.)* Do you think that this is the best decision for Willy to make at this time? (See Supplementary Activity #3.) Do you have some suggestions for her as to what she should do to "look out for herself"?

Supplementary Activities

1. Willy mentions on page 123 that the year is 1782. Find out what was happening in your area in 1782. Visit the local Historical Society and/or library. Do some research. Dramatize life as it was there in 1782.

---

2. Find out what else was going on in 1782. The following is a sample of the events of that year. Do some research about one of these events, or of something else that occurred at that time. Share your findings with others, or, if appropriate, include them in the dramatization of the life and times of your area.

1782

a) The Great Seal of the United States, with the motto *"E Pluribus Unum,"* was adopted.

b) The giving of the Purple Heart medal to those wounded in battle was initiated by George Washington.

c) Martin Van Buren was born in Kinderhook, New York.

d) Holland recognized the independence of the United States.

e) Americans battled Indians at Sandusky, Ohio.

f) The U.S. and France agreed upon a repayment plan at Versailles for the war loan.

g) The United States and England signed preliminary articles of peace in Paris.

h) The French army embarked from Boston.

i) James Monroe became a member of the Virginia Assembly.

j) Washington urged state governors to pay sums to support Congress.

k) Vermont accepted conditions of admission to the Union.

l) The presidio and military town of Santa Barbara, California was founded.

m) The British House of Commons resolved against further war in North America.

n) The British Parliament acted to enable the king to make peace with America.

o) Sir Guy Carleton was sent from England to America to carry out peace conditions.

p) John Jay and John Adams joined Ben Franklin in Paris to negotiate peace.

q) Thomas Jefferson estimated the cost of the war at $140 million.

r) The entire foreign debt at this time was $7,885,085.

s) The first Bible was printed in the United States in Philadelphia.

t) The song "Yankee Doodle" first appeared in print.

u) Samuel Stearns published the first nautical almanac in America.

v) The Harvard Medical School opened.

w) Washington College in Maryland was the first to be named in George Washington's honor.

3. Mr. Goodrich brings some news to Willy. What does he tell her? *(Pages 131-132, He tells Willy that her mother is alive, but very ill.)* What will Willy decide to do? Make a prediction. However, in doing so, weigh the consequences of going back to Captain and Mrs. Ivers.

Chapter 12—Pages 133-161

Vocabulary

rouse 137   dory 152

Vocabulary Activity

How many words can you rhyme with the vocabulary words?

Rouse: house, blouse, mouse...

Dory: lory (parrot), glory, story, hunky-dory (fine)...

Make up a plausible sentence that uses as many of the rhyming words as possible. For example: A girl named Lori read a hunky-dory story about a lory that won glory while out on a dory.

Discussion Questions and Activities

1. What is the story of Willy's mother? *(Page 141, Willy's mother was kept on a ship for two years to wash clothes for the officers. She got sick, and her health fluctuated from then on, as she was sometimes better, sometimes worse. When the peace treaty was signed, she was let off of the ship on Long Island. Uncle Jack was notified, and he came to get her, and brought her to the home of Captain Ivers.)* If you were Ma, what would you tell Willy to do?

2. Willy goes to get the doctor. What is the reason that the doctor gives to Willy for not going to see her mother? What does the doctor do instead? *(Page 146, "I can't go into a man's house if he doesn't want me there." The doctor gives Willy some medicine for her mother.)* What is your opinion of the doctor's reply regarding the visit to the house? Discuss the right of an individual to determine who may enter his/her house. (See Supplementary Activity #2.)

3. After Ma dies, Willy starts to run away, but then comes back to the Ivers' house (page 153). Why do you think that she returns?

Supplementary Activities

1. Uncle Jack tells Willy of his dilemma regarding Captain Ivers. Willy thinks, "Well, it was a terrible thing. It seemed like the black folks was bound to lose, no matter what happened" (page 142). Do some research. Does the Declaration of Independence address the problems of the slaves? *(The Declaration of Independence contained no provision for the manumission of the slaves. Two months after the Declaration, Massachusetts issued a proclamation calling slavery "utterly inconsistent with the struggle for liberty." Within the year, several Massachusetts towns abolished slavery. In the years following, Jefferson worked out an elaborate law for gradual emancipation and removal of Negroes from Virginia, but neither he nor any of his colleagues ever submitted it to the Virginia legislature. However, for black people, the War for Independence had little or no immediate meaning.)*

2. Invite a retired lawyer in to speak to the group regarding the law(s) that govern the rights of individuals in their homes, and who may enter and under what circumstances.

3. Do you think that Mr. Goodrich will be able to help Uncle Jack? Make a prediction.

Chapter 13—Pages 163-169; Chapter 14—Pages 171-173

Vocabulary

petition 163   testify 165   manacles 166   implicit 167
manumitted 167   pipsqueak 168

Vocabulary Activity

Do the vocabulary word search puzzle, page 29 of this guide.

Discussion Questions and Activities

1. Check your prediction. Is Mr. Goodrich able to help Willy's Uncle Jack? What happens? *(Pages 167-169, Jack Arabus and Wilhelmina Freeman are both given papers stating that they are free.)* What do you think would have been the result of the assault charge had that been pursued? On what do you base your opinion?

2. Why does Willy want to go back to New York? *(Page 172, "There was more of a chance of doing what I wanted to do there.")* Do you agree with Willy? Do you think that New York will be different than other places for a free, black woman? Why or why not?

Supplementary Activity

On page 172, Willy is thinking about freedom. "But I could see that nobody was free all the way. There wasn't nobody who could do anything he wanted...Captain Ivers couldn't keep me and Uncle Jack in slavery; and Mr. Fraunces, he had to do what his customers wanted; and Mr. Goodrich took his orders from the judge; and the judge—well, I didn't know what his limit was, but I reckoned that he had one. They was all stuck one way or another. It was just that some people was way down at the bottom of the heap and a lot more stuck than others." Brainstorm the word FREEDOM. Has our understanding of freedom changed much today? Discuss.

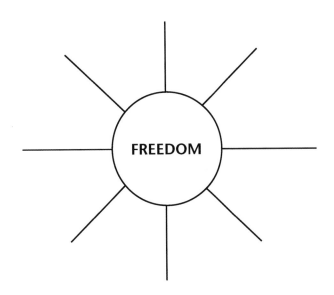

Post-reading Activities

1. Fort Griswold: History records that on September 6, 1781, while General Washington was leading the French and American armies into Virginia to trap Lord Cornwallis at Yorktown, a band of British soldiers sailed up the Thames River in Connecticut to burn the towns of Groton and New London. The redcoats were led by the American traitor, Benedict Arnold. Two men saw the enemy boats, a white farmer named Latham and his black slave Lambert Latham. The two men ran to join other Americans at Fort Griswold under the leadership of Colonel William Ledyard. Arnold's men surrounded the fort, and finally entered it. Ledyard handed over his sword to a British officer, who took it and ran it through Ledyard's body to the hilt. Lambert Latham, who was standing by the commander, turned on the British officer and stabbed him with his bayonet. Many British soldiers then slashed the slave until he died with 33 wounds in his body.

   More than 50 years later, when the state of Connecticut put up a marker in honor of the 84 patriots killed by the British raiders on that September day, the name of Colonel Ledyard was placed at the top, followed by the names of 81 other whites. At the bottom, under the heading "Colored Men," were the names of Latham and Freeman, two slaves. The name of the brave Lambert Latham, who had been known by the nickname of "Lambo," had been carved in marble as "Sambo."

   Imagine that you are Lambert Latham, speaking from the grave. You quote the Declaration of Independence and say, "We hold these Truths to be self-evident, that all men are created equal..." Continue on to tell what you think of the marker put up in the honor of all of the men who gave their lives at Fort Griswold in order that the Declaration of Independence could be implemented.

2. Cipher Continued: Cipher—The mathematical symbol denoting absence of quantity (0); zero. A number. Any cryptographic system in which units of plain text of regular length, usually letters, are arbitrarily transposed or substituted according to a predetermined key. (code) To put a message in secret writing.

Code Key														
Letter	A	B	C	D	E	F	G	H	I	J	K	L	M	N	O
Becomes	X	Y	Z	A	B	C	D	E	F	G	H	I	J	K	L
Letter	P	Q	R	S	T	U	V	W	X	Y	Z			
Becomes	M	N	O	P	Q	R	S	T	U	V	W			

Solve by using the code key: **TFIIV COBBJXK FP X DFOI.** *(WILLY FREEMAN IS A GIRL.)*

Create your own letter substitution table. Make up a sentence or question that has to do with the story. Share with others in the group.

Can you figure out how to solve this in a different way? (Each word is written by putting letters in order last to first.) **YMRA SPOORT DNA AITILIM ERA TA TROF DLOWSIRG.** *(ARMY TROOPS AND MILITIA ARE AT FORT GRISWOLD.)* Follow a different pattern for mixing letters. Make up a message from the content of the story.

3. Problem Solving/Logic: Willy and Horace will make some stew to serve. What will they use in the stew? If they have beef, potatoes, and carrots what are the possible combinations of ingredients to put into the pot? (**b** = beef, **p** = potatoes, **c** = carrots)

b	**b + p**	**b + p + c**
p	**b + c**	
c	**p + c**	

Add tomatoes to the choices. (**t** = tomatoes) All of the above plus **t**. (Check with others in the group to determine if additions are necessary to your list.)

t	**t + b**	**t + b + c**	**t + b + p + c**
	t + c	**t + b + p**	
	t + p	**t + p + c**	

Add more ingredients, and list the choices. Do you notice a pattern developing?

Add rice to the choices. (**r** = rice) All of the above plus **r**. (Check with others in the group to determine if additions are necessary to your list.)

r	**r + b**	**r + b + p**	**r + b + p + c**	**r + p + b + c + t**
	r + p	**r + b + c**	**r + b + p + t**	
	r + c	**r + b + t**	**r + c + b + t**	
	r + t	**r + p + c**	**r + p + t + c**	
		r + c + t		
		r + t + p		

4. Immoral Weapons: In the twentieth century, certain weapons are considered immoral. There were also weapons considered immoral in the Revolutionary War. In 1775, one British officer suggested putting smallpox germs on arrowheads and shooting them at Americans. His superiors would not allow such action. In the summer of 1776, British soldiers claimed that the Continental soldiers were quartering or halving musket balls. This kind of ammunition would fragment and tear the flesh once it hit the body. Wounds from such musket balls were more serious and far more painful than the wounds from unfragmented musket balls.

Surgeons would have an impossible task trying to repair the damage left to muscle and bone*. In addition, British General Howe wrote to General Washington, complaining that Continentals were firing lead bullets with the points of nails protruding from them. Washington claimed that the sample bullet sent to him by Howe was the first one that he had ever seen. He called the use of the bullet a "wicked and infamous practice." (*Are there bullets currently available that wound in a similar manner? Are they considered immoral?)

Why are some weapons considered immoral and others not? What makes a weapon fit into the category of "immoral"? What is your opinion of immoral weapons?

5. The *Turtle*: Use the following information about the *Turtle* to create:

- a class play for dramatization
- an article for the local newspaper
- a manual for the operation of the submarine
- a fictional story based on fact
- something of own choice

David Bushnell, while a student at Yale University, built the world's first submarine. The vessel was called the *Turtle*, and it operated by a hand-cranked propeller. It ran at a rate of approximately three miles an hour in still water. On the submarine was an explosive magazine containing 130 pounds of gunpowder that the submarine pilot could attach to an enemy vessel. An army sergeant named Ezra Lee took the submarine under the waters of New York Harbor in August of 1776. The mission was to sink a British warship anchored there. The mission took place late at night. The submarine was towed close to the British fleet by two whaling boats. Lee battled strong tides only to find that he was unable to attach the magazine to the British ship. Although the mission was not successful, the *Turtle* made it to shore safely.

Vocabulary Word Search Puzzle

Do the word search. Write down the letters that have not been used, starting at the top, and working left to right in each row. Group the letters into words to find the hidden message.

```
A  R  G  U  M  E  N  T  A  T  I  V  E  W  K  M
P  M  C  A  L  C  U  L  A  T  I  N  G  I  E  A
O  C  O  C  K  A  D  E  H  I  T  H  E  R  E  N
T  A  R  N  L  O  Y  A  L  I  S  T  S  L  L  U
H  R  D  E  G  A  M  A  N  A  C  L  E  S  L  M
E  T  W  G  B  S  P  A  L  I  S  A  D  E  S  I
C  R  O  O  G  E  T  B  A  R  R  A  C  K  S  T
A  I  O  T  J  U  L  J  O  L  L  I  T  Y  C  T
R  D  D  I  F  O  N  S  S  A  W  Y  E  R  O  E
Y  G  W  A  E  R  L  N  C  U  R  T  S  Y  U  D
T  E  I  T  R  O  I  L  E  Y  Y  D  L  C  N  O
E  S  N  I  R  U  O  T  Y  L  O  O  K  I  D  R
T  P  D  O  Y  S  S  F  T  B  O  R  N  P  R  Y
H  I  L  N  H  E  E  R  M  E  O  O  T  H  E  H
E  K  E  S  A  U  N  T  E  R  R  A  E  E  L  R
R  E  D  E  T  E  R  M  I  N  E  D  T  R  S  X
```

ARGUMENTATIVE	AMONGST	NEGOTIATIONS	CLAPBOARD
PALISADES	SCOUNDRELS	LOYALISTS	GUNNEL
DWINDLED	MANACLES	JOLLITY	SAUNTER
APOTHECARY	CALCULATING	CORDWOOD	DETERMINED
COCKADE	REBELS	BARRACKS	MANUMITTED
CARTRIDGES	JOLLY BOAT	FRITTER	CURTSY
SAWYER	ROUSE	FERRY	DORY
CIPHER	KEEL	TETHER	HITHER
PIKE	YON		

29

American Revolution Word Search Puzzle

Do the word search. Write down the letters that have not been used, starting at the top, and working left to right in each row. Group the letters into words to find the hidden message.

```
R  E  V  O  L  U  T  I  O  N  A  R  Y  W  A  R
K  S  T  A  M  P  A  C  T  C  C  Y  L  I  D  B
I  J  A  G  L  T  W  I  L  O  A  O  E  N  E  O
N  L  O  R  U  L  E  Y  S  U  M  R  X  D  C  S
G  E  E  H  A  I  E  A  S  R  D  K  I  E  L  T
S  H  E  R  N  T  L  Y  A  T  E  T  N  P  A  O
M  F  O  R  T  P  O  F  F  C  N  O  G  E  R  N
O  H  I  L  L  F  A  G  O  O  T  W  T  N  A  M
U  B  U  N  K  E  R  U  A  R  R  N  O  D  T  A
N  C  O  N  C  O  R  D  L  A  D  G  N  E  I  S
T  R  E  N  T  O  N  T  H  J  E  R  E  N  O  S
A  K  T  I  C  O  N  D  E  R  O  G  A  C  N  A
I  B  R  A  N  D  Y  W  I  N  E  N  I  E  L  C
N  C  O  N  T  I  N  E  N  T  A  L  E  L  E  R
H  O  U  S  E  D  C  O  N  G  R  E  S  S  X  E
G  E  O  R  G  E  W  A  S  H  I  N  G  T  O  N
```

STAMP ACT	GUILFORD	REVOLUTIONARY WAR	BRANDYWINE
JOHN PAUL JONES	CONTINENTAL	CONGRESS	CONCORD
TEA ACT	YORKTOWN	GEORGE WASHINGTON	BUNKER
LEXINGTON	FORT	VALLEY FORGE	HILL
CAMDEN	SARATOGA	TICONDEROGA	INDEPENDENCE
BOSTON MASSACRE	DECLARATION	TRENTON	COURT
KING'S MOUNTAIN	HOUSE		

Vocabulary Crossword Puzzle

Match a vocabulary word, listed in Words Used, with its definition, listed under Across or Down. (Words Used: argumentative, bargain, bayonet, britches, cockade, furloughed, implicit, instructive, leastwise, magazine, massacre, musket, petition, populace, refugee, smithereens, squinch, straggling, suspicious, swivel, tether, tuppence.)

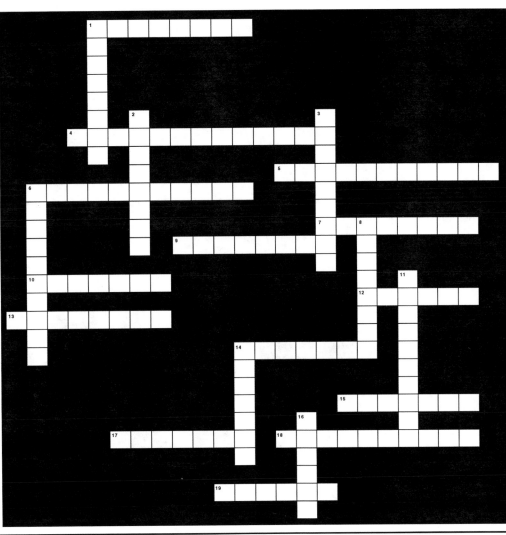

Across

1. Storeroom for ammunition
4. Given to arguing
5. Conveying information
6. Bits
7. Implied
9. Trousers
10. Rosette or knot of ribbon worn on a hat as a badge
12. Rope
13. Masses
14. Negotiate
15. Segment of building
17. Person seeking refuge
18. On a leave of absence
19. Pivot

Down

1. Indiscriminate killing
2. Coin worth two pennies
3. Anyway
6. Questionable
8. Formal written application
11. Falling behind
14. Knife on a gun
16. Shoulder gun

American Revolution Crossword Puzzle

Please Note: Full names do not have a space between the first and last names. Match a vocabulary word, listed in Words Used, with its definition, listed under Across or Down. (Words Used: Aaron Burr, Benedict Arnold, Bonhomme Richard, Boston, Continental, Count Pulaski, George, George Washington, Hessians, Independence, Lexington and Concord, Nathan Hale, Philadelphia, Saratoga, Thomas Paine, Valley Forge, Yankee Doodle, Yorktown.)

Across

2. Continental Army Commander in Chief
4. Song of the time
6. City of Liberty
7. Fighting breaks out in these two towns April 19,1775
12. Name of British King
13. Name of Polish general
15. City of Tea Party
17. German Mercenaries
18. Declaration of...

Down

1. Place in New York where Burgoyne surrenders
3. Location of miserable winter quarters for Washington's army
5. Name of John Paul Jones' ship
8. Later in life acquitted of treason charge
9. Name of first congress
10. Place where Cornwallis surrenders
11. Name of man who deserts to the British
14. Author of pamphlet "The Crisis"
16. Said, "I only regret that I have but one life to lose for my country."

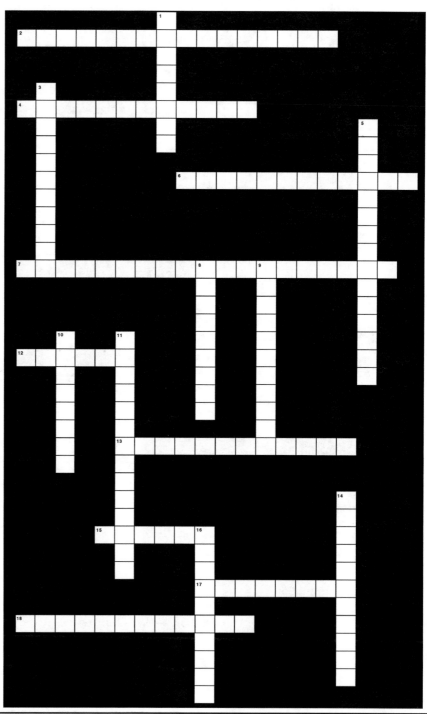

Teacher Information

Yankee Doodle

Few songs of the Revolutionary War era have survived the passage of time. "Yankee Doodle" and William Billings' "Chester" are possibly the only songs that are a legacy of the Revolution. At that time, no real musical base had been established in the Colonies. What music there was came largely from England. There was not a widespread circulation of music, and few could make a living as professional musicians. The religious background of many placed severe strictures against "entertainments." The origins of "Yankee Doodle" have been obscured by history. It was widely known as an instrumental melody by the middle of the eighteenth century, and was popular as a tune for dances and jigs. The words to the song have changed over time, but it is the only song left from the American Revolution, and is America's first national patriotic song. Even before the war began, many British people looked down on the American colonists. To people in Britain, the Americans seemed like poorly educated farmers who dressed in ill-fitting clothing and lacked good manners. The song was written by a British doctor who worked in America in 1758. The word "Doodle" is an English term meaning fool or simple-minded person. Janke, a Dutch name used by many settlers in the colonies, became the word Yankee. Therefore, a Yankee Doodle is a term of ridicule and scorn. Many of the British soldiers who came to America to fight sang the song to mock the Continentals. However, the Americans added their own words to the song during the Revolutionary War. The song was sung at the first Fourth of July celebration in Philadelphia in 1777.

"Yankee Doodle is the tune
Americans delight in;
It suits for feasts, it suits for fun,
And just as well for fighting."

Slaves for America

Many colonists who came to North America were to become closely entangled with the lives of the Africans who were brought there. The land of North America was plentiful and rich, and it didn't make sense for a colonist to work for somebody else when land down the road could be had for practically nothing. It became clear that what was needed in the new colonies was a supply of laborers whose ambitions could be limited. At first, debtors from England and Ireland were brought to the colonies to work off their debts. Criminals were also sent on the ships that left for the east coast of America. However, the need for labor was much greater than could be filled by people from Europe. Meanwhile, it was common practice among warring African nations that prisoners taken in battle were held in captivity for long periods of time. European traders eyed these captives, and saw in them an opportunity to solve the labor problem in the colonies. They began to trade their goods for African prisoners, and in 1619 the first African captives were brought to Virginia. At first there was little difference in the attitudes toward Africans and indentured whites. However, the laws of Great Britain protected the indentured servants by clearly stating how much time they had to serve, and declaring their children to be free. No such system protected the African captives. Some of the first Africans brought to this country were eventually freed under laws similar to indenture laws; most were not. Gradually those areas of the country that used the labor of African captives made laws saying that they would have to serve for as long as they lived, and their children would also have to serve forever. The Africans "belonged" to whoever held them captive. Once the trade in Africans started, it increased quickly. The raids on West Africa that supplied North America with labor lasted for 236 years, from 1619 to 1855, long after the legal importation of Africans had ended. America seemed to be the land where the poor could become rich. All that was needed was land and labor. Many of the early colonists seem to have seized the opportunity and the land from the Native Americans, while utilizing the labor of African captives.

American Revolution Timeline
— 1763 —
End of the French and Indian War.

Britain's King George issues proclamation to the American colonies forbidding westward expansion.
— 1765—
Parliament passes the Stamp Act.
— 1770 —
March 5: Five colonists die in what came to be known as the Boston Massacre, a street argument that got out of control. The first to fall is Crispus Attucks, a mulatto runaway slave.
— 1773 —
May 10: Tea Act
Dec. 16: Boston Tea Party is held in Boston Harbor as a rebellion against the Tea Act. Colonists board British ships and dump cargo of tea overboard.
— 1774 —
Sept. 5: The First Continental Congress opens in Philadelphia.
September: Rhode Island and Connecticut pass laws against the importation of Negroes into the colonies, but not against slavery.
October: Congress is asked, "...while we are attempting to free ourselves and preserve ourselves from slavery, that we also take into consideration the Negro slaves in this province." The request is not acted upon.
— 1775 —
First emancipationist society in the U.S. is organized in Philadelphia.
April 19: Fighting breaks out at Lexington and Concord, as British troops come to confiscate alleged military supplies. The "shots heard round the world" are fired.
May: Committee considering the use of Negro soldiers decides that only free men should be used because use of slaves would be "inconsistent with the principles that are to be supported."
May 10: Second Continental Congress opens, and recognizes a state of war exists and issues "Declaration of Causes for Taking up Arms." Americans capture Fort Ticonderoga.
June 6: A resolution sent to Congress recommends "that no slave be admitted into this army upon any consideration whatsoever."
June 15: George Washington is named Commander in Chief.
June 17: Battle of Bunker Hill (Breed's Hill), the bloodiest of the entire war
July 3: Washington takes control of the Continental Army, and among the troops are many black veterans of the French and Indian War as well as soldier-slave minutemen.
July 10: George Washington forbids recruiting of "any Negro" or "any Person who is not American born."

Sept. 26:	Southern states recommend discharge of all Negroes.
October 8:	Due to increasing participation of blacks, American generals agree "to reject all slaves" and "Negroes altogether."
Nov. 12:	General Washington again orders, "Neither Negroes, boys unable to bear arms, nor old men are to be enlisted."
Dec. 1:	Thomas Jefferson denounces slavery in original draft of Declaration of Independence.
Dec. 8:	News reaches General Washington of British governor's enlistment of slaves; Washington allows enlistment of free Negroes.
Dec. 30-31:	Americans fail to capture Quebec.

— 1776 —

Jan. 15:	General Washington authorizes the reenlistment of "free Negroes who have served faithfully in the Army at Cambridge but no others."
March 17:	British evacuate Boston.
June:	Thomas Jefferson submits an early draft of the Declaration of Independence; accusing the English King of participating in the slave trade. "He has waged cruel war against human nature itself, violating the most sacred rights of life and liberty in the persons of a distant people who never offended him, captivating and carrying them into slavery in another hemisphere or to incur miserable death in their transportation thither."
July 4:	The Declaration of Independence is signed by members of the Continental Congress and is published, omitting the reference to the slave trade.
August 17:	German mercenaries (Hessians) arrive in New York to fight for the British.
August 27:	British defeat the American army at New York's Long Island; this begins the war-long occupation of New York City by the British. Black soldiers participate.
Sept. 15:	British occupy New York.
October 28:	Battle of White Plains; black soldiers participate.
Nov. 16:	British capture Fort Washington.
Nov. 20:	British capture Fort Lee.
Nov. 26:	Battle of Trenton
Dec. 25:	Washington crosses the Delaware; black soldiers participate.
Dec.26:	Washington's troops surprise the Hessians, defeating them in the Battle of Trenton. Black soldiers participate.

— 1777 —

Vermont becomes the first state to abolish slavery. Virginia forbids the enlistment of any black without a "certificate of freedom." North Carolina prohibits the freeing of slaves except for "meritorious conduct."

January 3:	Battle of Princeton
June 14:	Congress adopts the "Stars and Stripes" flag.
July 6:	British capture Fort Ticonderoga.
Sept. 11:	Battle of Brandywine; blacks participate.
Sept. 19:	First Battle of Freeman's Farm
Sept. 26:	British occupy Philadelphia.
October 4:	Battle of Germantown
October 7:	British are beaten at Second Battle of Freeman's Farm.
October 17:	Burgoyne surrenders a large portion of the British army at Saratoga, New York. Blacks participate.

Nov. 15:	Articles of Confederation adopted by Congress and sent to states for ratification; privileges of citizenship given to "free inhabitants" only.
Dec.19:	Washington moves his army to miserable winter quarters at Valley Forge.

— 1778 —

Rhode Island authorizes enlistment of slaves.

February 6:	France and America sign an alliance.
June 28:	Battle of Monmouth; 700 blacks participate.
August 29:	Battle of Rhode Island; Colonel Green's newly authorized First Regiment of 125 blacks distinguishes itself by "deeds of desperate valor."
Nov. 11:	Butler's Rangers, aided by Mohawk Chief Joseph Brant, massacre settlers at Cherry Valley, New York.
Dec. 29:	British occupy Savannah, Georgia; blacks participate.

— 1779 —

Feb. 24:	George Rogers Clark and his small band of men capture the British fort at Vincennes on the Wabash River, and "Hair Buyer" Hamilton is sent to prison.
March 14:	As a result of the British campaign in the South, Alexander Hamilton, in a letter to Congress, urges greater use of blacks, saying: "The contempt we have been taught to entertain for the blacks, makes us fancy many things that are founded neither in reason nor experience...But it should be considered, that if we do not make use of them in this way, the enemy probably will."
March 29:	Congress urges South Carolina and Georgia to raise a battalion of slaves for which owners will be paid not less than one thousand dollars. The states refuse.
June 21:	Spain declares war on Britain.
June 30:	British General Clinton solicits black soldiers saying; "And I do promise to every Negro...who shall desert the Rebel Standard full Security."
July:	General Wayne's victory at Stony Point is helped by work of black spy, Armistead.
Sept. 23:	John Paul Jones's ship *Bonhomme Richard* captures the British ship Serapis in a bloody sea battle.
October 9:	Battle of Savannah; black Haitians from the French Fontages Legion save the French and American armies.

— 1780 —

May 12:	Americans under Benjamin Lincoln surrender at Charleston, South Carolina.
August 16:	Battle of Camden
October 7:	Over-mountain men soundly defeat the British and Loyalist troops at King's Mountain, North Carolina.

— 1781 —

New York promises freedom to all slaves who serve in the army for three years or until discharged. New Jersey prohibits slave enlistment. Maryland resolves to integrate 750 blacks with other troops. Negro troops under Colonel Green fight to the last man at the Battle of Point Bridge, New York.

March 15:	Battle of Guilford Court House
April 25:	British General Cornwallis begins his campaign to end the war quickly by taking Virginia.
August 14:	Washington, hearing French Admiral de Grasse is coming to Chesapeake Bay with a large naval force, makes plans to secretly send his army to Yorktown.
Sept.15:	French fight off British fleet in Chesapeake Bay.

Sept. 28:	Siege of Yorktown begins; blacks participate. British garrison at Fort Cornwallis also includes 200 blacks.
October 19:	Cornwallis surrenders at Yorktown, ending the British military threat in America.

— 1782 —

April 12:	The naval battle of the *Saintes* restores British command of the sea.
July 11:	British evacuate Savannah.
Nov. 30:	A preliminary peace treaty is signed in Paris.
Dec.14:	British evacuate Charleston.

— 1783 —

April 19:	United States ratifies preliminary peace treaty.
Sept. 3:	The final peace treaty signed in Paris formally ends the war.
Nov. 25:	The last British troops leave New York.

Puzzle Answers

Vocabulary Crossword Puzzle Answers, page 31

Across:
1. MAGAZINE
4. ARGUMENTATIVE
5. INSTRUCTIVE
6. SMITHEREENS
7. IMPLICIT
9. BRITCHES
10. COCKADE
12. TETHER
13. POPULACE
14. BARGAIN
15. SQUINCH
17. REFUGEE
18. FURLOUGHED
19. SWIVEL

Down:
1. MASSACRE
2. TUPPENCE
3. LEATWTIT... (grid letters: L E A T W)
6. SUSPICIOUS
8. PETITION
11. STRAGGLING
14. BAYONET
16. MUSKET

American Revolution Crossword Puzzle Answers, page 32

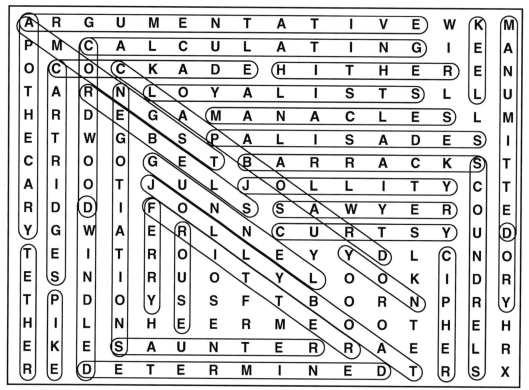

Vocabulary Word Search Puzzle Answers, page 29

(Hidden Message: WILLY LOOKS FOR HER MOTHER X)

American Revolution Word Search Puzzle Answers, page 30

(Hidden Message: WILLY SEES HER FATHER KILLED X)